T. GONDII

Poems by

NINA BELÉN ROBINS

Thompson & Columbus, Inc., Publishers
New York

ISBN:
978-0-9832275-6-4

Cover and Book Design
Mark Wedemeyer / Carbon13 Design Bureau

Cover Illustration
Mark Wedemeyer / Pixabay

www.thompsonandcolumbus.com

DEDICATED TO

Felix

Timothy
Thomas

Small Cat

Bobo

Minino

Moho

Tashi

Buster

Sheba

Musette

Silvey

Bruno

Cleopatra

Dottie

Dashie

Smallbit

Bean

&

Paisley

ALSO BY NINA BELÉN ROBINS

Supermarket Diaries

*A Bed With My
Name On It*

PREFACE

"How could you take this ability for granted?" insensitive people have asked Nina Belén Robins.

Well, they are talking about the wrong skill and to someone who takes nothing for granted and tells us so with such simple eloquence that you admire her way with words while she changes your outlook on life. We all wonder if we will grow old alone, if our love is gift enough. Nina asks us to ponder these universal questions at the same time she offers us a glimpse into a world of hardships not all of us have had to endure.

In this new collection she writes about her decision not to have children in poems ranging from heartbreaking to angry. She tears my heart with lines like "These are my babies; do you see how much I love them? They are forbidden from coming through. I do not have enough towels to sop up the blood." Poems about her battle to be sterilized make me angry for her and remind me I have to defend my freedom in a country where "a woman's body is public property unless a notary signs off on it."

"Oh perseverance!" Nina writes of her cats, her constant companions, who "only love when they want to. When they want to keep you alive, they stay up all night keeping watch, waiting to catch you." And this is how I understand her, from years of reading her poems, seeing her perform and knowing her personally. Pick up one of her books and expand your ideas about love and family.

—Laura Vookles, mother to human and cats

CONTENTS

T. GONDII

HOW THEY SHOW THEY CARE
(OR
HOW THEY SHARE THEY THINK I DON'T)

1. You'll change your mind when you get older. You're still so young. You'll see that I'm right.

2. When you meet the right guy you will want them.
   He'll convince you.

3. It's your purpose, as a woman. We have to perpetuate the human race. It's what you have to do.

4. Are you really that selfish that you refuse to care about anyone other than yourself?

5. You always complain about too much free time. If you had a child, it would fix that.

6. When you are an adult, you live through your child. It's the only way to have a fulfilling life.

7. I can't believe you would kill your child! No one goes through life never getting pregnant.

8. How could you not have children? There are so many women out there who can't have them. How could you take this ability for granted?

9. How about your parents? Don't they want grandchildren? How could you deprive them like that?

10. What are you going to do when you're old and alone? When you have no one to take care of you? No children to put you in a home? *What are you going to do when you have to die with no one to love you?*

My life is not empty without you, small one.

I'd know if it were.

I'd give up everything.

TO MY FUTURE MOTHER IN LAW

I hope that my love for your son will be enough;
my devotion to his happiness sufficient heart use.
He will never be lonely,
always held, listened to, understood.

I hope my heart, mind, skin are
enough organs to prove my commitment;
our four hands held together a family;
holiday cards sent to you in December
needing only two names.

My body wasn't built to build bodies.
My rollercoaster has too many hills
without a nine-month inescapable hormonal cyclone.

I will hold your son in sleep.
I need sleep, down time, peace and quiet.
I will love your son with love only a real woman feels.
We will visit for thanksgiving, take family portraits.

Too many mothers have thought me
incubator for their namesake,
it seems unavoidable, I am never spared.

I do not cheat, always hold, pay half for every date,
I'm learning how to cook. I listen, absorb,
have intellectual conversation,
please, love with all of me, don't know jealousy,
do not obsess, possess, claim, hold back.

I was not built to build bodies.
It is not in my makeup,
not an option.

I will give your son every other organ.

To my future mother in law,
I will give your son
sunsets, harvest moons, love.

I will give him myself,
family.

After everything I give him,
I hope you will be satisfied.

After everything I give you
I hope that it will be *enough*.

DARK SIDE

I want to marry Darth Vader so we use his picture,
pretend it's the Sith Lord.
My sister, ordained, we say, *I do.*

My teacher erased *Satan was here* from the chalkboard.
The kids at their desks snickered hard
at the braided girl who wrote it.

I ran from the Dean after cursing him,
he sprinted after me, tried to catch me.
I offered him my screech, I didn't have the force yet.

A 12-year-old girl has socked her mother
in the ear so many times she's deaf.
a 12-year-old girl has threatened to kill
the one who married her every night their entire lives.

A Skywalker without the control of the force.

We watch the movies in the theater.
He chokes a man with nothing more than
fingers grasping the air.
I grasp my sister's hair in my hands and pull,
slam the door!

A 12-year-old Sith Lord
slams the door to the Death Star,
winds up with the stars, dying, with no air.

ODE TO THE CAT APP IN MY PHONE

There is a cat who lives in my phone and I named her Dottie although I think she's supposed to be a boy cat named Tom but I had the option of naming her.

The strongest man at work has a cat in his phone too because lots of people like cats no matter how tough they are.

Cats.

She needs pets.

I'm sorry, I can't have sex with you right now. I have to pet my cat and feed her ice cream and she has to poop and this is what's important in life.

And she burps when I pet her too hard and I can relate.

I'm sorry, I can't bake cookies right now, I have to pet my cat.

Shh! My cat is sleeping. I pretend to let her sleep but I'm going to check on her in five minutes.

Nope, still sleeping.

If you ask me if your kid is cute I'll tell you no because she's not my cat in my phone. Even if your kid's cute. Nope, she's not.

Dottie loves me. I love Dottie.

I will never have children. No. I will have cat children. In my phone.

Damnit! My battery's dead. Dottie drained it. I bought a charger at the store and there has to be an outlet somewhere so I can pet her and feed her ice cream and put her to bed.

Like a real cat.
Like a child.

I'm sorry, were you talking? Dottie was asking for pets.

PUDDLE

He is leaving. The apartment is empty
except the air mattress.

I still love you he says.
We could be fated.

We could be When Harry Met Sally
in five years.

You'll be ready for children, then.
You keep getting better.

There's a house in Missouri waiting for you.
Two dogs, eventually our children.

We can give them a paper route.
They'll play soccer.

The air mattress keeps deflating.
I can feel the floor beneath my back.

I don't want children.
I don't want dogs.

Our future is a painting in a museum
only one of us is in.

Sunrise. He drives off.
His future son and daughter safely buckled in the back seat.

I am an empty womb, left on the floor.
No husband, no children, no house and no dogs.

The sun beats down and all the mothers
begin to emerge.

Open their jaws.
Feast on my carcass.

INDOOR CAT AND FORMER OUTDOOR CAT

1.

I didn't ask to be rescued,
here in this house with these creatures.
You, born in a cardboard box,
me in the field.

2.

They feed us canned food
as though the birds cannot
hear me through this imprisoning screen.
You, squeaking at the fly on the wall,
you do not know the language of the sparrow.

3.

If you, as I, had bathed in the showers
you run from when the loud noises erupt at us
on the window sill, you would not startle.

4.

I must tell you of the fields,
the human who lured me here.
Of the streams with the bugs
I have been taken from.

5.

One day I will teach you these tongues.
We will catch the door
with outstretched tail.

We will run, taste the fresh air,
feel the pavement.

We will be free.

7.
That sounds great!
Oh! Look! They're feeding us!

WOMB

Broken, empty womb,
useless as the appendix,
but ruptures monthly.

T. GONDII

Write a poem about cats, he says,
about the parasite in their feces,
how it's probably why you're crazy.

Explain how the crazy cat ladies
have T. Gondii from the litter.

Explain the symptoms.

When I was 10 I ran
into oncoming traffic when my cat died.

When I was 10
my teacher bought me a coffee table book
about cats.

My boyfriend and I don't want children
and there is cat furniture everywhere.

When I was 11
I tried to jump off a six-story building.
I used to clean the litter box every week.

Search the internet,
he tells me.
Explain why you're crazy.

How all the cat ladies start out as normal
then their hair turns crazy like yours.

He picks up our cats and narrates them,
built a house for Bean
because she likes to be contained.

Bleaches the litter box when I ask him to.
Needs a haircut.

Loves his cats.

BEAN

Bean meows just one meow,
7am every day.
Well trained, I give treats.

BREAK

When the condom broke last fall,
I couldn't tell. It felt the same.

I saw the tear, blinked our clothes on,
into the car, drug store,
I don't remember paying or what drink I chose,
just that I downed the whole thing;

we drove back to his place,
squeezed all night.

I cried, for three weeks at work.
They joke you know about him and me.
Marriage. Children.

Why wouldn't they?
We are good people,
love each other,
this seems to be a permanent thing.

Only now, I'd wind up on the bathroom floor,
a puddle of fluids, none that I was hoping for.

It is not my choice, despite all my boasting.
All the crude ways in which I would flush
the children down the toilet,
all the ways I'd terminate.

My cold womb nothing more than
an ejection seat awaiting its first use.

I cannot bear children.
Not on these meds,
not with these hormones,
genes, needs.

If he or she formed there was
nothing but evacuation,
nothing but rejection.

Love that I will never feel.

Love I have to shout out,
I DO NOT CARE IF I NEVER FEEL!

It does not matter if I care,
do not,
might,
might not,
might,
might not,

might.

THE VET MEETS ESPRESSO BEAN

What do you call her?

Bean/Baby Bean/Beantastic/Bean Baby/Beaneriffic/Fne/Little Bean/
Kitten/Sweet Baby/Sweet Pea/Little Angel/Sweet Thing/light of my life/
angel of my existence/daughter

You don't have kids, do you.

CONSENT.

What is your name?
Nina Belén Robins.

Were your rights read to you?
Check.

Do you know you can change your mind?
Check.

Do you know it won't be held against you?
Check.

What day were you born?
5/25/84

What day is today?
5/25/16

If your signature doesn't match your name,
they will refuse you. Say we forced you.
They're picky like that.

A woman's body is only her own if her name is spelled right.

It's permanent and you've been counseled.
Check.

I can't believe you're doing this on your birthday.
Check.

You're over 18.
Check.

You'll never be pregnant.
Check.

You can change your mind.
Check.

The notary is coming,
signing that we didn't tie you to a chair,
you weren't held here against your will.

I've been kept from this office against my will.

A woman's body is public property unless a notary signs off on it.

What a birthday present.
No kids.

I won't keep you long.
Check.

Sorry for the wait.
It's been 32 years.

Keep your phone around,
they'll call you, council.

Try to change my mind.
30 days to change my mind.

Push hard on the pen so the carbon paper works,
shows through, your decision etched on yellow paper.

A woman's body is only her own if the carbon paper works properly.

Don't tell anyone, no one will support you.

A woman's body isn't her own unless everyone supports her.

30 days.
No fallopian tubes.
A 32 year prison sentence

finally done.

LOVE

I've come home & opened the can of cat food & one of my kittens bolts down the stairs like they do when they hear this noise but my baby, the one who's always hungry, the spoiled one, (we don't have favorites. You don't have favorite children. But we have favorites. But we have favorite children) does not come down. He's under the bed whimpering & there is vomit & foam & my husband doesn't come home for another hour & as soon as he does we whisk him off to the nearest emergency room with its waiting room & x-rays & I sign the waiver that if he goes into cardiac arrest they can revive him (what sort of electric probes do you use on a six-month old kitten with his little belly and little furs that are still fuzz and his paws) & we sit there, I'm half medicated so nothing is quite registering because it's the time of day I'm supposed to not be conscious & they bring him out & *there's NOTHING wrong with him they say. He's fine. He didn't eat a nail & he didn't eat your anti-anxiety med & he didn't eat a stink bug & we took the x-rays & you owe us $700 will that be cash or credit?*

Once when I was 20 my vision went blurry & my parents put on their shoes at 11 pm & got on the train for 40 minutes & we sat for an hour in the waiting room of the emergency room in our coats with snow outside & they called me in to take my pressure & my sugar & *there was NOTHING wrong with me. It was an anxiety attack. I didn't have diabetes & I didn't have a brain tumor & I didn't have hypertension & I wasn't going blind & that'll be $700 will that be cash or credit?*

Nina will be fine tonight. You can go home. We gave her some water. You don't have to worry. Thank you for coming here. You are good parents. You are good parents.

Smallbit will be fine tonight. We gave him fluids. He isn't going to die. You are good parents. You are good parents.

You are.

ODE TO THE CAT SITTER

Oh cat sitter,
trusted one,
key holder,
food giver,
do not let the kittens go unfed.
Change the box,
throw the toys,
pet them,
close the door as you enter,
they do not know the wilderness.
Brush them,
talk to them,
make sure they are not lonely.
Search the house,
make sure they are not stuck somewhere.
Look for hairballs,
love them,
tell them we'll return soon
if they get lonely.
Promise.
Send pictures every day.

Please take care of them,
they are my children.

CHILDREN

The children have his blue eyes,
dimples from all of our cheeks.

The girl can sing in the shower better than I can,
the boy is shy.

We are all eating fettuccine alfredo.

Don't tell Grandma!
My daughter warns my son.

We are all in the park, they are growing.
They rollerblade like I did, bike.

The girl turns 11, wonders what death is;
another thing we have in common.

The boy is six-feet tall now,
like his father.

He slams the door, like I did,
holds a knife to me, like I did.

His sister stabs herself, like I did.
Her brother curses, like I did.

They both cry like I did,
beat like I did, scream like I did.

The house is collapsing like it always has.

I gather them back into my womb,
push them through, send them back,
screeching through the bloody doorway.

There are no children.

The nurse asks me why I'm being sterilized.

I open up my wallet,
let all the pictures fall to the floor.

These are my babies,
do you see how much I love them?
They are forbidden from coming through.
I do not have enough towels to sop up the blood.

THE NEW GIRL

When the girl came to live here,
fertile, unlike those of us who lived here all along,
with her calls to me in the night,

loud, as I slept
on the floor of the bedroom
where it's cool in the summer,

her calls
early in the morning
as I ate my breakfast.

This siren throughout the house
I'd never heard before, my loins lurching
(I did not know it a possibility; this longing)

pushing her lips on my face, rubbing me
until finally I caved,
our parents out doing whatever they do,
my sister upstairs napping.

Oh what sensation!
Mounting this woman!
The pleasure!

Daily, we make love.
Me, a man for the first time,
she, calling my name all night
until we sneak into the bedroom once more.

My love!
My lover!
My woman!
Purring and meowing me into heaven!

WOLVERINE

Wolverine and I have had a daughter.
She is on the movie screen.
I have never met Logan, but there she is,

looking like us,
brown hair, knives for hands.

My daughter is on the movie screen
and my lover is drinking his Snapple
like he doesn't know I've given birth without him.

Look my love, look at how they keep
her hands locked, like they kept my hands locked.
Look at how they try to quiet her.

She cuts her arms and my scars ache.
I bet she'd love me.
I bet I'd cover her with kisses until my knives came out,
we'd sword fight with fingers.

This is why I'm with you, and not Wolverine.
You have dull points. You have pads.

Wolverine and I have had a daughter,
she runs around the theater,
neither one of us can tell her
we didn't want her,
we want to love her but can't.

My tears fill up an empty bag of popcorn,
you comment on the gratuitous violence.
This is why we shouldn't have come to see the film.

That night,

I take a razor to my wrist and face,
lock myself in the bathroom,
feel where my fertility used to be,

feel where there will never be a baby.

She'd claw her way through my womb,
anyway.

You grab me by the wrist,
unscrew the doorknob from the door.

I fall asleep.

The credits roll down the screen.
There is no daughter in the bed upstairs.

LOVE AFFAIR

She gazes out the window,
he slinks over to lick her neck,
blows in her ears, so she stretches
by the window sill, bats her eyes.
This is soft love.
She mellows, rolls over.
He bites her neck,
scratches down her back.
Birds outside peeking in
now that she's distracted.
She tolerates this until his teeth dig too deep.
Not now! She hisses. Swats his face.
Falls to the floor, tail up.
We can't do this! You have no balls!
I'm never in the mood anymore they took my hormones!
He chases her up the stairs
until she runs under the bed.
I shake the food dish to distract him,
it works, his hunger is constant
for more than just sex.
She climbs back onto the window sill.

He forgets she's there.

PMS

When I am not throwing
coffee tables at the window,
he tells me not to worry about
him leaving me.

The three weeks in the month
when the cats are on our laps
like the children we pretend they are,
Guy Fieri is eating pulled pork,
I have iced tea brewing in the kitchen
we paid to share last June.

When the black eye I gave myself
last week has cleared up,
his tears have been wiped away,
he tells me to think
of him holding me tonight when he comes to bed.

He says,
I know it wasn't you who threw the plate at me,
missing my face and shattering
against the cabinet,
scaring the cats upstairs.
This is why I know you can fix it.
Do not think about my leaving.

Go to the doctor.
Fix yourself.

I go upstairs and think
of every door I've swung
off the hinges,

every scar I've left,
how if I were a man
this would not be PMS, but abuse.

The gentle creature
downstairs playing with the cats,
two weeks until my ovaries
make me hate him again;

the quiet threat of being alone again
humming in the heater;
knowing he cannot stand this forever.

How do you not think
about a fist whose only talent is undoing things.

PAISLEY

Paisley destroys the house.
We joke I birthed her,
because two of us now
knock things off the table
in fits of rage.

The loosest of gun barrels, us two.
The rebels of the house.

My boulder of a husband
on the couch wondering
who will destroy what,
the slight fear of finding
either of us dead from some act,
accidental or intentional.

Last week I came home to meowing,
found a five pound cat
puddled behind the fridge.

Once I stayed a day
at my husband's job
because if left to my own
workings I'd be gone.

Now there is a cat on my lap,
on the bed,
because what is more
in life than knowing
there is a constant
keeping you here,

covered in fur
or otherwise.

SMALLBIT'S HAIKU

Nft#*@ jkhgb
Yf643(hujnv
$&szkponnb

JESUS

The therapist sits
across from me;
crossed legs,
dimples,
frosted brown hair.

He sits there after telling me
a poem about Jesus as a scenario for therapy
in which HE is Jesus,
we're walking along the beach.
His footprints don't show,
but that doesn't mean he doesn't love me.

This is our second session.

You know, some would say
God wants you to have bipolar children.
How does your family feel?
They have depression;
those are their genes.
Surely this decision hurts them.

My family says bipolar people
are talented so people want to fuck us
and that's why we still exist.

Jesus is silent.
The clock on the wall
reads that the session is over.

Another egg jumps off the ledge
where the tubes used to be,

absorbed by the time I've left the building.

MIGHTY BRAVE KNIGHT

Oh cat!
Oh hunter!
Oh mouse droppings behind the stove!
Oh might!
Oh strength!
Oh hours spent staring at the crevices!
Oh pitter of paws!
Oh smell of fur!
Oh wait!
Oh stare!
Oh hours in the kitchen!
Oh scamper from stove to fridge!
Oh scamper from fridge to stove!
Oh patience!
Oh perseverance!
Oh humans!
Oh work day over!
Oh television!
Oh stench!
Oh wonderment!
Oh search!
Oh rot!
Oh find!
Oh carcas!
Oh retch!
Oh paper towel!
Oh disposal!
Oh hunter!
Oh brave!
Oh proud!
Oh gross!

DAUGHTER

I dreamt last night I had a daughter.
I've had motherhood dreams before,
ending in pregnancy,
losing the pregnancy.

She was seven, pretty, brown hair like mine,
we lived in Nyack.

My daughter didn't have a name,
was seven, brown hair like mine,
bipolar, already cutting.

I loved her with love
I've never felt in real life,
held her, told her not to cut,
it wasn't worth it.

She looked at my arms.
You have scars too.

Yes, I know pain.
Yes, I'm no virgin to pain.

I held her.
She still had cuts on her arms.

In reality, I know these things are genetic.
I have these issues from genes,
but in my dream what a shock it was,
my sadness passing
from my womb into another person,
seeing her self destruct
at the same young age
my destruction took place.

When people ask me why I don't want children
I explode with excuses
but the truth is
my sadness is as much in my womb
as it is my heart.

My kin were suicidal,
I was suicidal.

There don't need to be any more
generations in my family
who want their parents at their burial.

My daughter was seven.
She had brown hair like mine.
We lived in Nyack.

We had the same brown eyes, smile.
The same scars.

WONDERFUL MOTHER

I forgot to brush my teeth again & there's clothes all over the floor & I slept through the alarm & I cried at work & I had to keep everything in & I was too tired to exercise & I had to take my medicine early last night so I was knocked out by 7:30 & I don't know how to cook & all my energy goes to not losing my temper every day & I had an anxiety attack that my husband had an affair & I had an anxiety attack that my parents died & I had an anxiety attack that the cats got out & I gag when I try to do the litter so he does it & I gag when the cats have a hairball & today I almost fell asleep at work & sometimes going from 6am to 8pm as a functional human is the hardest journey I've ever been on & today was especially bad so I'm laying on the couch under the blanket with Smallbit & don't even have the energy to open the can of cat food so I ask him to do it.

I'd make a terrible mother. The kids would starve. I couldn't even change a diaper.

I think they'd die.

It's ok, Nina. Take your medicine. Go to sleep. It doesn't matter. I don't care. I'll feed the cats. I'll do some laundry. I'll be up in a few hours. Take it easy. We don't need children. We have each other. You are enough for me. I'll never ask you for anything more.

BEDTIME

Two cats, toy rabbits,
an anxiety blanket.
Husband off the hook.

THERAPY CAT

I've jumped off a building, gone to hell.
(It's always hell when I jump,
when I'm shot I usually see
some deceased grandparent who feeds me,
tells me I need to stop dying
every night,
need to stay on earth and feel alive.)

This time I've fallen
off a nine-story building,
I must have shrieked so loud,
because my face is being washed
by my kitten,
suddenly I'm in bed again.

I wonder how many calories
I burn running from one end of the bed to the other.
I've had men refuse to sleep next to me,
but I wake up and my kitten
is purring and holding my hand.

There's some blood pressure medicine
that cures night terrors,
(pharmaceuticals like making drugs
that cure more than one thing,
claim to cure more than one thing,
try to convince us we have more than one thing,)
which they try to give me,
I think I'm ok with my cat for now.

Carrie Fisher carried her dog everywhere,
a cat isn't docile like that.
Just licks my face and purrs,
holds my hand every time I die.

If you read an article about cats,
it'll tell you purring lowers blood pressure.
Cats only love when they want to.

When they want to keep you alive,
they stay up all night keeping watch,
waiting to catch you.

ACKNOWLEDGMENTS

I would like to acknowledge my parents and husband who sat in the waiting room all day while I got my sterilization surgery, fixed me my favorite meal for dinner, and never even once questioned my decision or tried to belittle me for making it, all the while fully understanding how painful it was to finally go through with it.

"Puddle" and "Jesus" first appeared in the lit mag "Anti Heroin Chic."

MY CATS ARE MY LIFE,
AND I KNOW SO MANY FEEL THE SAME WAY.

With all the natural disasters, animals being left behind because of various life circumstances, and animal cruelty in general, animals need all the help they can get.

I don't know what I'd do without my cats, so one dollar from every sale of this book will be donated to the ASPCA.

You can find out more about the ASPCA here:

www.aspca.org

PRAISE FOR *A BED WITH MY NAME ON IT*

Bookended by movingly hopeful poems, this collection carries the reader into places we may never have been and may hope never to go to. But having been there and come through—with the writer—with humor, deep humanity, and an energizing self-acceptance, we're better for it. These poems have the music of performance poetry in them and the power of crafted literary work. We have here a very satisfying and rare merger of talent, humility and valuable life experience. No poem fell flat for me. Every poem invites and rewards multiple readings. — *Elizabeth K. Gordon*

❖

If you have ever had a moment that made you feel out of control, this book has a poem for you. Several, in fact, and not one of them gives you a feeling of anything less than survival at its finest.

Don't forget this poet's name. Nina will have a long career.

You won't forget the poetry. — *Wil Gibson*

❖

I read this book in one sitting! Nina brought us into her life and spread light into so many places so often left in the dark. It was a pleasure to share her perspective. I work with girls in a community residence and I could relate to each page with the girls I have worked with as well as my own personal experiences. This was so powerful. — *Amanda*

❖

Nina's book *A Bed with my Name on It* is tragic beauty. The poems are filled with so much raw emotion, each one is like a gut punch of "damn." I'm very grateful for her poems. — *Nick Yuk*

A BED
WITH MY
NAME
ON IT

Nina Belén Robins

This book of poems draws on the
author's experience within the
mental health system from the
time she was a little girl until she
reached her early twenties. The
poems illuminate the soul-numb-
ing degradations that spurred her
to find her way out of the system
and the kindnesses that made it
possible.

PRAISE FOR *SUPERMARKET DIARIES*

This magnificent volume of poetry is the author's first published
book but surely not her last. With impeccable insight and a vivacious
appreciation for the human condition, Robins takes us on a journey
behind the supermarket check-out counter. She offers us a unique
glimpse into the lives of the ordinary people who cross her path each
day, using her incredible poetic talents to convince us of the extra-
ordinary humanity of each of them, and by extension, of ourselves.
I highly recommend this book! — *choirqueer*

Simple observations, expressed with great insight, wisdom
and eloquence. — *Dan Couture*

In a variety of stories through the eyes of a creatively observant
cashier, Nina's writing is sharp witted, emotional, and promises to
be very memorable! — *Zadra*

This is *The Spoon River Anthology* of supermarkets: insightful
poems about customers, staff and life behind the cash register,
by an exciting young NYC poet. Can't wait for the next book!
— *Lori Ubell*

SUPER-MARKET DIARIES

Nina Belén Robins

Mild-mannered grocery store employee by day, Nina Robins is a well-known performance poet who has twice performed at the National Poetry Slam. Her poetry has been described as "exceptionally appealing," "heartbreakingly honest," and "subversively deep for work so overtly entertaining."

—Taylor Mali, author of
What Teachers Make

Nina Belén Robins is a three-time National Slam Poet, and author of the books of poetry, *Supermarket Diaries* and *A Bed With My Name On It.* She spent much of her life in various institutions, but has finally broken free and lives with her husband and cats, working in the bakery department of a supermarket. She writes whenever possible, and wants to help normalize and destigmatize mental illness as best she can.

CPSIA information can be obtained
at www.ICGtesting.com
Printed in the USA
JSHW062012300822
29806JS00005B/122